THE LITTLE BOOK OF
PROSECCO
AND SPARKLING COCKTAILS

First published in Great Britain in 2022 by Pyramid,
an imprint of Octopus Publishing Group Ltd
Carmelite House, 50 Victoria Embankment, London EC4Y 0DZ
www.octopusbooks.co.uk

Distributed in the US by
Hachette Book Group
1290 Avenue of the Americas
4th and 5th Floors
New York, NY 10104

Distributed in Canada by
Canadian Manda Group
664 Annette St.
Toronto, Ontario, Canada M6S 2C8

ISBN 978-0-7537-3509-1

A CIP catalogue record for this book is available from the British Library

Printed and bound in China

10 9 8 7 6 5 4 3 2 1

Publisher: Lucy Pessell
Designer: Hannah Coughlin
Editor: Sarah Kennedy
Editorial Assistant: Emily Martin
Production Manager: Serena Savini

The measure that has been used in the recipes is based on a bar jigger, which is
25 ml (1 fl oz). If preferred, a different volume can be used, providing the
proportions are kept constant within a drink and suitable adjustments are made to
spoon measurements, where they occur.

Standard level spoon measurements are used in all recipes.
1 tablespoon = one 15 ml spoon
1 teaspoon = one 5 ml spoon

This book contains cocktails made with raw or lightly cooked eggs. It is prudent
for more vulnerable people to avoid uncooked or lightly cooked cocktails made
with eggs.

INTRODUCTION
4

FLUTES
6

HIGHBALLS
30

ROCKS & WINE GLASSES
44

MARTINIS AND COUPETTES
68

JUGS & BOWLS
72

BAR BASICS & TECHNIQUES
86

INDEX
96

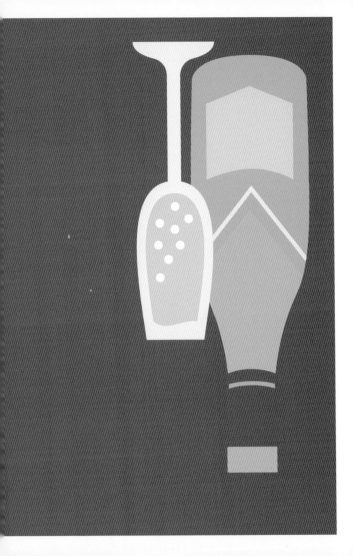

PROSECCO IS THE ANSWER. WHAT WAS THE QUESTION?

Now we're all down with Prosecco being every bit as delicious as Champagne (it's fruitier and more floral) and actually just plain better than Champagne (it's cheaper), it's time to let it work its magic in our cocktails.

With classics like the Champagne Cocktail, modern twists like the Mojto Royale and Passionfruit Spritz, and brilliantly bubbly concoctions that put Prosecco centre stage like the Rossini and the Sunshine State, this book has a deliciously drinkable cocktail for everyone for every occasion.

So, whether you're looking for something bubbly for a boozy brunch, something fabulously fizzy to fire-up a Friday night or something sophisticated for a special moment, *The Little Book of Prosecco and Sparkling Cocktails* has it all.

FLUTES

DUSK TILL DAWN

1 measure gin

¼ measure crème de pêche

¼ measure Aperol

¼ measure lemon juice

Prosecco, to top

rose petal, to garnish

Add all the ingredients except the Prosecco
to a cocktail shaker and fill with cubed ice.

Stir for 30 seconds, and strain into a Champagne flute.

Top with chilled Prosecco and garnish with a rose petal.

BELLINI

½ ripe white peach

dash sugar syrup

Prosecco, to top

Add the peach and sugar syrup to a blender or
food processor and blend until smooth.

Pour into a Champagne flute and top with
chilled Prosecco.

ORCHARD BELLINI

½ ripe white peach

1 measure apple juice

dash sugar syrup

Prosecco, to top

Add the peach and sugar syrup to a blender or food processor and blend until smooth.

Pour into a Champagne flute with the apple juice and top with chilled Prosecco.

FLORAL
BELLINI

½ measure rose liqueur

1 teaspoon lavender syrup

2 measures grapefruit juice

Prosecco, to top

dried lavender flowers, to garnish

Pour the rose liqueur, lavender syrup and grapefruit juice into a cocktail shaker filled with cubed ice.

Stir for 10 seconds and strain into a Champagne flute.

Top with chilled Prosecco and garnish with dried lavender flowers.

AMBIKA
BELLINI

4 slices mango

2 teaspoons grenadine

Prosecco, to top

Add the mango and grenadine to a blender or food processor and blend until smooth.

Pour into a Champagne flute and top with chilled Prosecco.

KIR ROYALE

1 measure crème de cassis

Prosecco, to top

Pour the crème de cassis into a Champagne
flute and top with chilled Prosecco.

RIVIERA
FIZZ

1½ measures sloe gin

½ measure lemon juice

½ measure sugar syrup

Prosecco, to top up

lemon, to garnish

Add all the ingredients except the Prosecco
to a cocktail shaker, shake vigorously and
strain into a chilled Champagne flute.

Top with Prosecco, and garnish with a lemon twist.

COBBLER
FIZZ

1 measure Fino sherry

3 slices mandarin

2 raspberries, plus extra to garnish

2 teaspoons sugar syrup

4 measures Prosecco

Add the mandarin, raspberries and sugar
syrup to a cocktail shaker and muddle.

Add the sherry and shake, then strain into a Champagne
flute before topping up with the Prosecco.

Garnish with a raspberry.

CELEBRATION
COCKTAIL

1 measure Cognac

1 teaspoon crème de mûre

1 teaspoon Bénédictine

1 lemon wedge

caster sugar, for frosting

Prosecco, to top

Frost the rim of a Champagne flute by moistening it with the lemon wedge and dipping it in the caster sugar.

Add the Cognac, crème de mûre and Bénédictine to the glass and top with chilled Prosecco.

BUCKS FIZZ

2 measures fresh orange juice, chilled

1 measure sloe gin, chilled

2 measures Prosecco

orange twist, to garnish

Add all the ingredients to a Champagne
flute and garnish with an orange twist.

CHAMPINO

1 measure Campari

1 measure sweet vermouth

Prosecco, to top

lemon, to garnish

Add the Campari and sweet vermouth to a
Champagne flute.

Top with chilled Prosecco and garnish with a lemon twist.

DEVIL'S
ADVOCATE

½ measure Campari

1 measure blood orange juice

½ measure sugar syrup

Prosecco, to top

orange, to garnish

Add all the ingredients except the Prosecco
into a cocktail shaker filled with cubed ice.

Stir for 10 seconds and strain into a Champagne flute.

Top with chilled Prosecco and garnish with a
twist of orange.

MANDARIN 75

1 measure Cointreau

½ measure lemon juice

2 teaspoons sugar syrup

Prosecco, to top

orange, to garnish

Add all the ingredients except the Prosecco
to a chilled Champagne flute.

Top with chilled Prosecco and garnish with an
orange twist.

FRENCH 75

1 measure gin

3 teaspoons lemon juice

3 teaspoons sugar syrup

4 measures Prosecco

lemon twist, to garnish

Add all the ingredients except the Prosecco
to a cocktail shaker and shake.

Strain into a Champagne flute and top with the
chilled Prosecco.

Garnish with a lemon twist and serve.

ZAN LA CAY

½ measure crème de pêche

1 teaspoon lemon juice

2 cubes cucumber

1 green cardamom pod

Prosecco, to top

cucumber, to garnish

Muddle the cucumber and cardamom in a cocktail shaker and then add all the ingredients except the Prosecco

Shake well and strain into a Champagne flute.

Top with chilled Prosecco and garnish with a slice of cucumber.

RUBY
TUESDAY

1 measure rum

½ measure lime juice

½ measure sugar syrup

6 raspberries

Prosecco, to top

raspberry, to garnish

Add the rum, lime juice, sugar syrup and raspberries to
a blender or food processor and blend until smooth.

Pour into a Champagne flute and top with
chilled Prosecco.

Garnish with a raspberry.

NEHRU

1 measure gin

4 slices mango

5 pink peppercorns

Prosecco, to top

Add all the ingredients except the Prosecco to a blender or food processor and blend until smooth.

Strain into a Champagne flute and top with chilled Prosecco.

ROSSINI

4 strawberries

1 teaspoon sugar syrup

Prosecco, to top

Add the strawberries and sugar syrup to a blender
or food processor and blend until smooth.

Pour into a Champagne flute and top with
chilled Prosecco.

HIGHBALLS

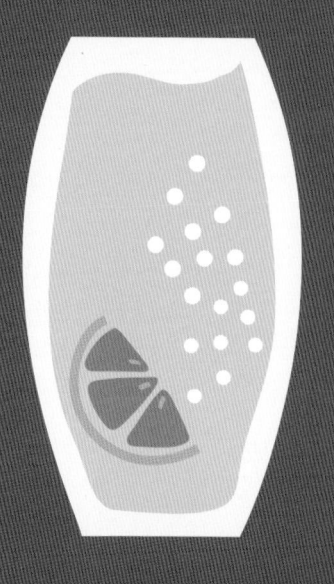

LOS
ALTOS

2 measures tequila

½ measure lime juice

2 measures orange juice

3 teaspoons agave syrup

2 teaspoons Campari

Prosecco, to top

orange and lime, to garnish

Add all the ingredients except the Prosecco
to a cocktail shaker, shake and strain into a
highball glass filled with cubed ice.

Top with chilled Prosecco and garnish with
a lime wedge and a slice of orange.

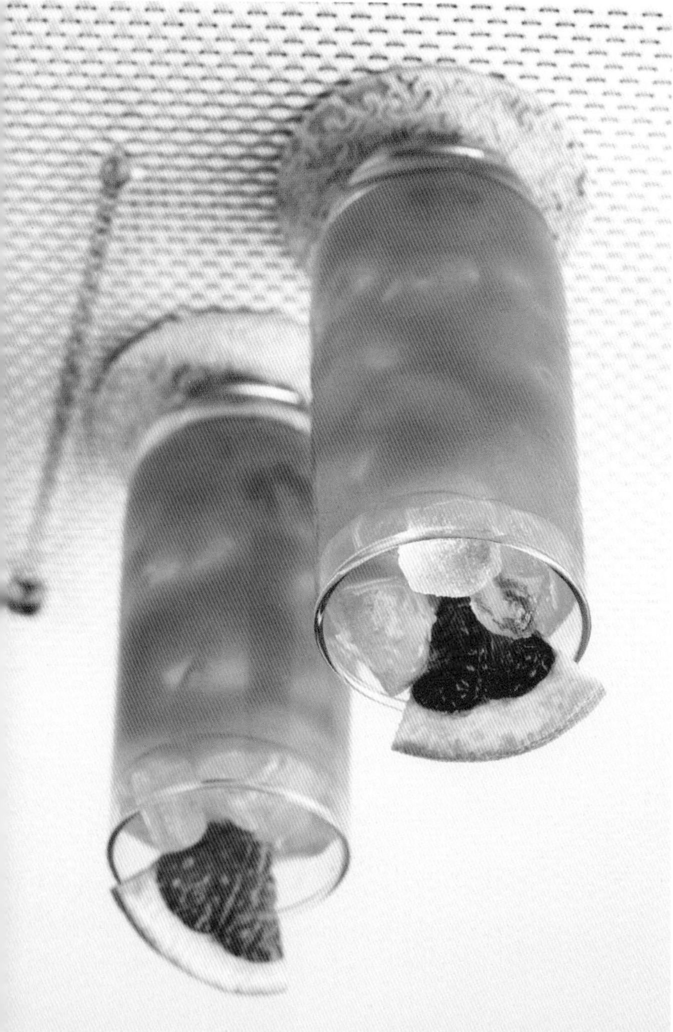

FRESH
PALOMA

1 measure tequila

2 teaspoons agave syrup

2 measures fresh grapefruit juice

Prosecco, to top

grapefruit, to garnish

Add all the ingredients to a highball glass filled with
cubed ice, stir well and garnish with a slice of grapefruit.

MOJITO
ROYALE

1½ measures white rum

8 lime wedges

2 teaspoons caster sugar

8 mint leaves

Prosecco, to top

mint, to garnish

Muddle the mint, sugar and limes in a
highball glass, add the rum and stir well.

Fill the glass with crushed ice, and churn vigorously.

Top with more crushed ice and chilled
Prosecco, and garnish with a mint sprig.

MONTECARLO
SLING

1 measure Cognac

1 measure peach liqueur

1 measure orange juice

Prosecco, to top

orange, to garnish

Pour the Cognac, peach liqueur and orange juice into a highball glass filled with cubed ice.

Top with chilled Prosecco and garnish with a slice of orange.

PROSECCO
JULEP

1 measure Cognac

8 mint leaves

1 teaspoon sugar

Prosecco, to top

mint, to garnish

Add all the ingredients except the Prosecco to a julep
mug or highball glass filled with crushed ice and churn.

Top with chilled Prosecco and more crushed
ice and garnish with mint sprigs.

ROYAL
COBBLER

1 measure gin

½ measure raspberry syrup

½ measure lemon juice

1 measure pineapple juice

Prosecco, to top

raspberries and mint, to garnish

Add all the ingredients to a highball glass
filled with crushed ice, and churn vigorously
until a frost begins to form on the glass.

Top with more crushed ice and chilled Prosecco, as
needed, and garnish with raspberries and a mint sprig.

SUNSHINE STATE

1 measure gin

½ measure elderflower liqueur

2 teaspoons lemon juice

1 measure apple juice

6 mint leaves

Prosecco, to top

strawberry slices, to garnish

Squeeze the mint leaves in your hand to express
the oils, then drop them into a highball glass.

Add the gin, elderflower liqueur, lemon juice and
apple juice, fill with cubed ice and stir well.

Top with chilled Prosecco, stir, and
garnish with the strawberry.

GOLDEN
APRICOT

1 measure rum

½ measure apricot liqueur

½ measure lime juice

2 teaspoons sugar syrup

Prosecco, to top

lime, to garnish

Add all the ingredients to a highball glass
filled with cubed ice and stir well.

Top with chilled Prosecco and garnish with a lime wedge.

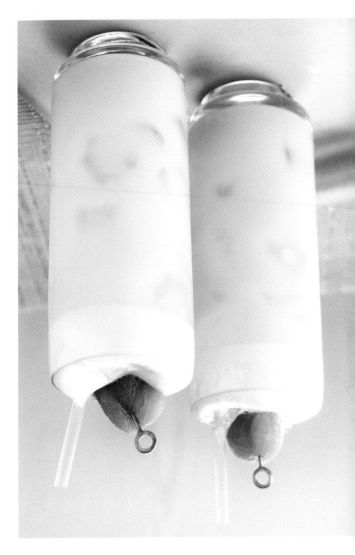

FRENCH
AFTERNOON

1 measure gin

½ measure lemon juice

1 measure camomile tea, chilled

¾ measure sugar syrup

Prosecco, to top

lemon, to garnish

Add all the ingredients except the Prosecco to a cocktail shaker, shake well and strain into a highball glass.

Top with chilled Prosecco and garnish with a lemon twist.

NEW DAWN
COOLER

1 measure vodka

2 measures apple juice

½ measure passion fruit syrup

Prosecco, to top

white grapes, to garnish

Add all the ingredients except the Prosecco
to a highball glass filled with cubed ice.

Stir well, top with chilled Prosecco and garnish with
white grapes.

ROCKS & WINE GLASSES

LYCHEE AND APEROL

2 measures Aperol

2 measures lychee juice

Prosecco, to top

orange, to garnish

Add the Aperol and lychee juice to a wine glass filled with cubed ice.

Stir well, top with chilled Prosecco and garnish with a slice of orange.

PINK
SANGRIA

2 measures rosé wine

1½ measures pomegranate juice

2 teaspoons agave syrup

Prosecco, to top

pink grapefruit, to garnish

Add all the ingredients except the Prosecco
to a wine glass filled with cubed ice.

Stir briefly, top with chilled Prosecco and
garnish with a slice of pink grapefruit.

PASSIONFRUIT
SPRITZ

1 measure vanilla vodka

1 measure passion fruit syrup

½ measure lemon juice

Prosecco, to top

mint and passionfruit, to garnish

Add all the ingredients except the Prosecco
to a wine glass filled with cubed ice.

Stir well, top with chilled Prosecco and garnish
with half a passion fruit and a sprig of mint.

PEACHES
AND GREEN

1 measure vodka

1 measure green tea, chilled

½ ripe white peach

1 teaspoon lemon juice

dash sugar syrup

Prosecco, to top

Add all the ingredients except the Prosecco to a
blender or food processor and blend until smooth.

Pour into a wine glass filled with cubed
ice and top with chilled Prosecco.

LA ROCHELLE
PUNCH

1 measure Cognac

1 measure Chambord

½ measure lemon juice

½ measure sugar syrup

Prosecco, to top

**raspberries, blueberries and blackberries,
to garnish**

Add all the ingredients except the Prosecco
to a rocks glass filled with cubed ice.

Stir well, top with chilled Prosecco and garnish
with raspberries, blueberries and blackberries.

SAKURA
PUNCH

1 measure vodka

1 measure lychee juice

1 measure grapefruit juice

2 teaspoons rose syrup

Prosecco, to top

grapefruit and cocktail cherry, to garnish

Add all the ingredients except the Prosecco to a rocks glass filled with cubed ice, stir well and top with chilled Prosecco.

Garnish with a slice of grapefruit and a cocktail cherry.

SBAGLIATO

1 measure Campari

1 measure sweet vermouth

2 measures Prosecco

orange, to garnish

Add all the ingredients to a rocks glass filled with cubed
ice, stir briefly and garnish with a slice of orange.

BITTER SPRING SPRITZ

1 measure Aperol

2 measures grapefruit juice

Prosecco, to top

grapefruit, to garnish

Add the Aperol and grapefruit juice to a
rocks glass filled with cubed ice.

Stir briefly, top with chilled Prosecco and
garnish with a grapefruit wedge.

G & TEA
SPRITZ

½ measure strawberry liqueur

1 teaspoon lemon juice

1 teaspoon sugar syrup

2 measures Earl Grey tea, chilled

Prosecco, to top

mint, to garnish

Add all the ingredients except the Prosecco
to a wine glass filled with cubed ice.

Top with chilled Prosecco and garnish with a mint sprig.

PARASOL

¾ measure gin

¾ measure lychee liqueur

¼ measure lemon juice

¼ measure sugar

Prosecco, to top

lemon and mint, to garnish

Add all the ingredients in a large wine glass
full of cubed ice, stir briefly and garnish with
a lemon wedge and a sprig of mint.

PRIMROSE
FIZZ

½ **measure elderflower cordial**

1 measure apple juice

6 mint leaves

Prosecco, to top

apple, to garnish

Squeeze the mint leaves in your hand to express the oils, then drop them into a wine glass.

Add the elderflower cordial and apple juice, fill with cubed ice and top with chilled Prosecco.

Stir briefly and garnish with apple slices.

COTTER
KIR

2 teaspoons crème de cassis

2 teaspoons raspberry liqueur

1 measure cranberry juice

Prosecco, to top

raspberries, to garnish

Add all the ingredients except the Prosecco to a
wine glass filled with cubed ice and stir briefly.

Top with chilled Prosecco and garnish with raspberries.

MELON
SPRITZ

1 measure melon liqueur

½ measure Aperol

2 measures soda water

Prosecco, to top

mint, to garnish

Add the melon liqueur, Aperol and soda water
to a wine glass filled with cubed ice.

Top with chilled Prosecco and garnish with a mint sprig.

HONEYDEW

1 measure gin

½ measure lemon juice

½ measure sugar syrup

2 drops absinthe (or Pernod)

5 cubes honeydew melon

Prosecco, to top

lemon and rosemary, to garnish

Add all the ingredients except the Prosecco to a blender or food processor and blend with 5 cubes of ice.

Pour into a chilled wine glass, top with chilled Prosecco and garnish with a lemon twist and sprig of rosemary.

SPICE
ROUTE PUNCH

1 measure Cognac

1 teaspoon cinnamon

½ measure lemon juice

½ measure sugar syrup

2 measures ginger ale

Prosecco, to top

cinnamon stick and apple, to garnish

In a glass, combine 1 measure Cognac with 1
tsp of cinnamon and leave for 10 minutes.

Strain the Cognac into a wine glass filled with cubed ice,
and add the lemon juice, sugar syrup and ginger ale.

Top with chilled Prosecco, stir, and garnish
with a cinnamon stick and slices of apple.

BLACKWOOD BLUSH

2 measures grapefruit juice

2 measures rosé wine

2 teaspoons crème de mûre

Prosecco, to top

grapefruit and thyme, to garnish

Add all the ingredients except the Prosecco
to a wine glass filled with cubed ice.

Top with chilled Prosecco, stir well and garnish
with a slice of grapefruit and a sprig of thyme.

CUCUMBER RANGOON

1 measure Pimm's No.1 Cup

2 measures cucumber juice

2 teaspoons ginger juice

2 teaspoons sugar syrup

Prosecco, to top

cucumber, to garnish

Add all the ingredients except the Prosecco
to a wine glass filled with cubed ice.

Top with chilled Prosecco and garnish with a slice
of cucumber.

MARTINIS & COUPETTES

AIRMAIL

1 measure white rum

½ measure lime juice

1 teaspoon honey

Prosecco, to top

Add all the ingredients except the Prosecco
to a cocktail shaker and shake well.

Strain into a chilled coupette glass and top with
chilled Prosecco.

CLASSIC CHAMPAGNE
COCKTAIL

1 measure brandy

1 sugar cube

1–2 dashes Angostura bitters

Champagne or Prosecco, to top

orange slice, to garnish

Saturate the sugar cube with the bitters, then drop it into a chilled martini glass.

Add the brandy, top with chilled Champagne or Prosecco and garnish with an orange slice.

SOUTHSIDE ROYALE

1½ measures gin

¾ measure lime juice

¾ measure sugar syrup

6 mint leaves

Prosecco, to top

mint, to garnish

Add all the ingredients except the Prosecco
to a cocktail shaker, shake vigorously and
double strain into a chilled martini glass.

Top with chilled Prosecco and garnish with a mint leaf.

JUGS &
BOWLS

HEDGEROW
PUNCH

3 measures sloe gin

1 measure crème de cassis

2 measures lemon juice

2 measures grapefruit juice

2 measures sugar syrup

Prosecco, to top

blackberries and mint, to garnish

Add all the ingredients to a jug or punch
bowl filled with cubed ice and stir well.

Garnish with blackberries and sprigs of mint.

BLUSH SANGRIA

4 measures vodka

2 measures raspberry liqueur

4 measures cranberry juice

2 measures lime juice

1 measure sugar syrup

Prosecco, to top

edible flowers, to garnish

Add all the ingredients to a jug or punch
bowl filled with cubed ice and stir well.

Garnish with edible flowers.

WHITE
SANGRIA

4 measures vodka

6 measures apple juice

2 measures lemon juice

2 measures elderflower cordial

4 measures soda water

Prosecco, to top

apple, lemon and mint, to garnish

Add all the ingredients to a jug filled
with cubed ice and stir well.

Garnish with the apple, lemon slices and sprigs of mint.

PARISIAN
FIZZ

2 measures raspberry purée

4 measures passion fruit juice

2 measures sugar syrup

1 measure Pernod

1 bottle Prosecco

raspberries and mint, to garnish

Add all the ingredients to a punch bowl
filled with cubed ice and stir well.

Garnish with raspberries and sprigs of mint.

TINTO
VENEZIA

4 measures Aperol

4 measures pink grapefruit juice

4 measures orange juice

4 measures rosé wine

Prosecco, to top

orange and grapefruit, to garnish

Add the Aperol, grapefruit juice, orange juice and
rosé wine to a large jug filed with cubed ice.

Stir well and top with chilled Prosecco.

Garnish with slices of orange and grapefruit.

LOLA'S
PUNCH

3 measures white rum

3 measures lemon juice

3 measures apple juice

3 measures mango juice

3 measures sugar syrup

4 measures soda water

Prosecco, to top

mango and apple to garnish

Add all the ingredients to a jug or punch
bowl filled with cubed ice and stir well.

Garnish with slices of mango and apple.

WATERMELON PUNCH

3 measures vodka

1 measure strawberry liqueur

8 measures watermelon juice

2 measures lime juice

2 measures sugar syrup

1 handful mint leaves, torn

Prosecco, to top

watermelon, mint and strawberry, to garnish

Add all the ingredients to a jug or punch
bowl filled with cubed ice and stir well.

Garnish with slices of watermelon, whole
strawberries and sprigs of mint.

BLUEGRASS
PUNCH

4 measures bourbon

3 teaspoons orange marmalade

2 measures lemon juice

1 measure sugar syrup

4 measures soda water

Prosecco, to top

orange, to garnish

Add all the ingredients to a jug or punch
bowl filled with cubed ice and stir well.

Garnish with orange slices.

BAR BASICS & TECHNIQUES

THE BASICS

Good cocktails, like good food, are based around quality ingredients. As with cooking, using fresh and homemade ingredients can often make the huge difference between a good drink and an outstanding drink. All of this can be found in department stores, online or in kitchen shops.

Ice

This is a key part of cocktails and you'll need lots of it. Purchase it from your supermarket, or freeze big tubs of water, then crack this up to use in your drinks. If you're hosting a big party and want to serve some punches, which will need lots of ice, it may be worthwhile finding if you have a local ice supplier that supplies catering companies, as this can be much more cost-effective.

Citrus juice

It's important to use fresh citrus juice in your drinks; bottled versions taste awful and will not produce good drinks.

Store your fruit out of the refrigerator at room temperature. Look for a soft-skinned fruit for juicing, which you can do with a juicer or citrus press. You can keep fresh citrus juice for a couple of days in the refrigerator, sealed to prevent oxidation.

Sugar syrup

You can buy sugar syrup or you can make your own. The most basic form of sugar syrup is made by mixing caster sugar and hot water together, and stirring until the sugar has dissolved. The key when preparing sugar syrups is to use a 1:1 ratio of sugar to liquid. White sugar acts as a flavour enhancer, while dark sugars have unique, more toffee-like flavours that work well with dark spirits.

BASIC SUGAR SYRUP RECIPE

Makes 1 litre (1¾ pints)

1 kg (2 lb) caster sugar

1 litre (1¾ pints) hot water

Dissolve the caster sugar in the hot water.

Allow to cool.

The sugar syrup will keep in a sterilized bottle stored in the refrigerator for up to two weeks.

CHOOSING GLASSWARE

There are many different cocktails, but they all fall into one of three categories: long, short or shot. Long drinks generally have more mixer than alcohol, often served with ice and a straw. The terms "straight up" and "on the rocks" are synonymous with the short drink, which tends to be more about the spirit, often combined with a single mixer at most. Finally, there is the shot which is made up mainly from spirits and liqueurs, designed to give a quick hit of alcohol. Glasses are tailored to the type of drinks they will contain.

Champagne flute

Used for Champagne or Champagne cocktails, the narrow mouth of the flute helps the drink to stay fizzy.

Champagne saucer

A classic glass, but not very practical for serving Champagne as the drink quickly loses its fizz.

Margarita or Coupette glass

When used for a Margarita, the rim is dipped in salt. Also used for daiquiris and other fruit-based cocktails.

Highball glass

Suitable for any long cocktail, such as a Long Island Iced Tea.

Collins glass

This is similar to a highball glass but is slightly narrower.

Wine glass

Sangria is often served in one, but they are not usually used for cocktails.

Old-Fashioned glass

Also known as a rocks glass, this is great for any drink that's served on the rocks or straight up.

Shot glass

Often found in two sizes — for a single or double measure. They are ideal for a single mouthful.

Balloon glass

Often used for fine spirits. The glass can be warmed to encourage the release of the drink's aroma.

Hurricane glass

Mostly found in beach bars, used for creamy, rum-based drinks.

Boston glass

Often used by bartenders for mixing cocktails, good for fruity drinks.

Toddy glass

A toddy glass is generally used for a hot drink, such as Irish Coffee.

Sling glass

This has a very short stemmed base and is most famously used for a Singapore Sling.

Martini glass

Also known as a cocktail glass, its thin-neck design makes sure your hand can't warm the glass or the cocktail.

USEFUL EQUIPMENT

Some pieces of equipment, such as shakers and the correct glasses, are vital for any cocktail enthusiast. Below is a wish list of things to have to hand for anyone who wants to regularly make decent cocktails.

Shaker

The Boston shaker is the most simple option, but it needs to be used in conjunction with a Hawthorne strainer. Alternatively you could choose a shaker with a built-in strainer.

Measure or jigger

Single and double measures are available and are essential when you are mixing ingredients so that the proportions are always the same. One measure is 25 ml or 1 fl oz.

Mixing glass

A mixing glass is used for those drinks that require only a gentle stirring before they are poured or strained.

Hawthorne strainer

This type of strainer is often used in conjunction with a Boston shaker, but a simple tea strainer will also work well.

Bar spoon

Similar to a teaspoon but with a long handle, a bar spoon is used for stirring, layering and muddling drinks.

Muddling stick

Similar to a pestle, which will work just as well, a muddling stick, or muddler, is used to crush fruit or herbs in a glass or shaker for drinks like the Mojito.

Bottle opener

Choose a bottle opener with two attachments, one for metal-topped bottles and a corkscrew for wine bottles.

Pourers

A pourer is inserted into the top of a spirit bottle to enable the spirit to flow in a controlled manner.

Food processor

A food processor or blender is useful for making frozen cocktails and smoothies.

Equipment for garnishing

Exotic drinks may be prettified with a paper umbrella and several long drinks are served with straws or swizzle sticks.

TECHNIQUES

With just a few basic techniques, your bartending skills will be complete. Follow the instructions to hone your craft.

Blending

Frozen cocktails and smoothies are blended with ice in a blender until they are of a smooth consistency. Be careful not to add too much ice as this will dilute the cocktail. It's best to add a little at a time.

Muddling

A technique used to bring out the flavours of herbs and fruit using a blunt tool called a muddler.

1. *Add chosen herb(s) to a highball glass. Add some sugar syrup and some lime wedges.*

2. *Hold the glass firmly and use a muddler or pestle to twist and press down.*

3. *Continue for 30 seconds, top with crushed ice and add the remaining ingredients.*

Shaking

The best-known cocktail technique and probably the most common. Used to mix ingredients thoroughly and quickly, and to chill the drink before serving.

1. *Half-fill a cocktail shaker with ice cubes, or cracked or crushed ice.*

2. *If the recipe calls for a chilled glass add a few ice cubes and some cold water to the glass, swirl it around and discard.*

3. *Add the ingredients to the shaker and shake until a frost forms on the outside.*

4. *Strain the cocktail into the glass and serve.*

Layering

Some spirits can be served layered on top of each other, causing lighter spirits to float on top of your cocktail.

1. *Pour the first ingredient into a glass, taking care that it does not touch the sides.*

2. *Position a bar spoon in the centre of the glass, rounded part down and facing you. Rest the spoon against the side of the glass as your pour the second ingredient down the spoon. It should float on top of the first liquid.*

3. *Repeat with the third ingredient, then carefully remove the spoon.*

Stirring

Used when the ingredients need to be mixed and chilled, but also maintain their clarity. This ensures there are no ice fragments or air bubbles throughout the drink. Some cocktails require the ingredients to be prepared in a mixing glass, then strained into the serving glass.

1. *Add the ingredients to a glass, in recipe order.*

2. *Use a bar spoon to stir the drink, lightly or vigorously, as described in the recipe.*

3. *Finish the drink with any decoration and serve.*

Double-straining

To prevent all traces of puréed fruit and ice fragments from entering the glass, use a shaker with a built-in strainer in conjunction with a hawthorne strainer. A fine strainer also works well.

INDEX

Airmail 69

Ambika Bellini 13

Bellini 8

Bitter Spring Spritz 55

Blackwood Blush 65

Bluegrass Punch 84

Blush Sangria 74

Bucks Fizz 19

Celebration Cocktail 18

Champino 20

Classic Champagne Cocktail 70

Cobbler Fizz 16

Cotter Kir 60

Cucumber Rangoon 66

Devil's Advocate 21

Dusk Till Dawn 7

Floral Bellini 11

French 75 24

French Afternoon 42

Fresh Paloma 33

G & Tea Spritz 56

Golden Apricot 40

Hedgerow Punch 73

Honeydew 63

Kir Royale 14

La Rochelle Punch 50

Lola's Punch 80

Los Altos 31

Lychee and Aperol 45

Mandarin 75 23

Melon Spritz 61

Mojito Royale 34

Montecarlo Sling 35

Nehru 27

New Dawn Cooler 43

Orchard Bellini 10

Parasol 57

Parisian Fizz 77

Passionfruit Spritz 48

Peaches and Green 49

Pink Sangria 47

Primrose Fizz 58

Prosecco Julep 36

Riviera Fizz 15

Rossini 28

Royal Cobbler 38

Ruby Tuesday 26

Sakura Punch 52

Sbagliato 53

Southside Royale 71

Spice Route Punch 64

Sunshine State 39

Tinto Venezia 79

Watermelon Punch 83

White Sangria 76

Zan La Cay 25